HAU KOLA
HELLO FRIEND

by

Paul Goble

photographs by

Gerry Perrin

MEET THE AUTHOR

Richard C. Owen Publishers, Inc.
Katonah, New York

Meet the Author titles

Verna Aardema *A Bookworm Who Hatched*
David A. Adler *My Writing Day*
Frank Asch *One Man Show*
Joseph Bruchac *Seeing the Circle*
Eve Bunting *Once Upon a Time*
Lynne Cherry *Making a Difference in the World*
Lois Ehlert *Under My Nose*
Jean Fritz *Surprising Myself*
Paul Goble *Hau Kola Hello Friend*
Ruth Heller *Fine Lines*
Lee Bennett Hopkins *The Writing Bug*
James Howe *Playing with Words*
Johanna Hurwitz *A Dream Come True*

Karla Kuskin *Thoughts, Pictures, and Words*
Thomas Locker *The Man Who Paints Nature*
Jonathan London *Tell Me a Story*
George Ella Lyon *A Wordful Child*
Margaret Mahy *My Mysterious World*
Rafe Martin *A Storyteller's Story*
Patricia McKissack *Can You Imagine?*
Patricia Polacco *Firetalking*
Laurence Pringle *Nature! Wild and Wonderful*
Cynthia Rylant *Best Wishes*
Seymour Simon *From Paper Airplanes to Outer Space*
Jean Van Leeuwen *Growing Ideas*
Jane Yolen *A Letter from Phoenix Farm*

Text copyright © 1994 by Paul Goble
Photographs copyright © 1994 by Gerry Perrin

Richard C. Owen Publishers, Inc.
PO Box 585
Katonah, New York 10536

Library of Congress Cataloging-in-Publication Data

Goble, Paul.
    Hau kola-hello friend by Paul Goble: photographs by Gerry Perrin .
    p . cm . -(Meet the author)
    Summary: An autobiographical account of prominent author/illustrator
Paul Goble and how his daily life and creative process are interwoven.

    ISBN 1-878450-44-1
    1 . Goble, Paul - Biography - Juvenile literature .
2 . Authors , American - 20th Century - Biography - Juvenile literature .
3 . Children's literature - Authorship - Juvenile literature .
[1 . Goble, Paul.   2 . Authors , American .
3. Children's literature - Authorship.   4. Indians in literature .]
I . Perrin, Gerry, ill . II . Title . III . Title : Hello freind ,
IV .Series : Meet the author (Katonah , N . Y .)
PS3557.02176Z47   1994
813 ' . 54—dc20
[B]   93-48167

Printed in the United States of America

9 8 7 6 5

Hau kola! Hello friend!
Is there a place outdoors
where you like to be quiet and think?
Perhaps it is at the riverbank where you fish,
or under a certain tree.
When I was growing up, I used to go to the lake
at the end of our garden.
I got to know that place in all its moods,
and every detail about it:
the trees, flowers, birds, and insects.
I would go there to think,
and the place helped me to grow up in my mind.

We lived in England,
near Oxford.

My father made harpsichords
and other musical instruments.
My mother was a musician.

I spent much of my time in search of wild flowers
for my pressed-flower collection,
and watching birds, of which I kept records.
I looked for stone-age tools and arrowheads
when the fields were newly plowed.
I drew and painted birds and butterflies
from books in our home,
and from specimens in museums.

I collected stamps and coins,
and I had a "museum" of rocks,
horseshoes, and feathers.
I grew up during World War II,
and so I also collected bullet shells
and pieces of German bombs,
two of which fell so close
that our house had to be re-roofed twice.

Always my greatest interest was in
everything related to Indian people.
I read all the books about them which I could find.
I was encouraged in this, as in all things,
by my mother.
She read me books about Indians,
and made me a tipi, and painted it with designs,
and sewed a fringed shirt and leggings for me to wear.
I now live in the United States, and
I still love those things from my childhood.
I feel fortunate that my family likes them, too.

Please meet my beloved wife, Janet,
and our son, Robert.
Our home is in Lincoln, Nebraska,
on a quiet street by a park.

In the morning
Robert feeds his
rabbit, Arthur,
and walks to
school.

Janet and I wave him
goodbye,
and then work starts.

We work at home, and so our house
is a little like a workshop.
I have a long desk at which I do
my writing and illustrating.
I work facing a window,
through which I see the park.
I also design my books,
and so I have a drawing table
to do accurate, measured drawing
for the layouts of the pages.
Janet creates a good feeling in the house.
Often I ask her advice:
"Does this paragraph sound all right?"
"What color should this be?" Sometimes I ask,
"Can you bring me a cup of tea, please?"

She is always thoughtful and encouraging.
People sometimes think that artists and writers
just wait for inspiration.
I have to work every day, and for long hours.
Some days it seems all work and little inspiration,
and I seem to cross out
everything that I write.
I use pen and pencil because
I cannot be creative
when using a machine.
I have an old-fashioned
typewriter just to copy
what I have written so that I
can read it better.

When I am drawing and painting,
I work with the same equipment
that I used when I was young:
pens, pencils, and watercolors.
Drawing is very difficult.
A day's work may have little to show
except messy drawings which I have rejected.

If I come across a problem that I cannot solve,
I walk in the park.
Every day I like to walk about four miles.
My thoughts seem to clear
when I have no roof over my head.
In the British Army, I was a good marcher
in the King's Shropshire Light Infantry!
Quite often the looked-for inspiration
comes while walking.
The way around the problem becomes clear.
It is a good feeling, but I think it only happens
because the hard work was done first in the studio.

As I work, I listen to classical music.
Bach is my favorite composer.
I grew up in a musical family.
Robert and I play duets on recorders which
my father made during the 1930's and 1940's
when I was young.

When I retell and illustrate an Indian legend
or a moment of history, I want to visit the people
and see the places I write about.

Janet, Robert, and I camp in beautiful and remote places in the Rocky Mountains, or out on the Great Plains of the Dakotas, Nebraska, Wyoming, Montana, and Alberta, Canada.

We meet Indian people who live there.

Janet is often the driver; she drives slowly because
I am likely to suddenly tell her "STOP!"
Perhaps I have seen a flower which I want to draw;
perhaps I have spotted a bird,
or need to photograph a butte.
This is the kind of information that I need later
in the studio when I am drawing.

I often make a quick sketch rather than
take a photograph, because
to draw something makes you look at it closely.
Those who know the Great Plains will recognize
some of the hills and buttes,
birds and plants in my books.

I write about things which happened long ago.
I try to get details right in my stories
and illustrations, because mistakes would be rude
to Indian people, and to my readers.

I may need to know the colors
and designs of blankets made a
hundred years ago, or the
designs that were painted
on rawhide storage bags.
I have my own library to
refer to.
I also have albums of
photographs, which I have
taken over the years,
of Indian artifacts in museum
collections.

When I am working on retelling a traditional
myth or legend, I often ask Indian people
to tell me the story.
I want to hear them tell it in their own words.
Sometimes they cannot because the memory of it
died with their grandparents.
I always have a lot of questions in my mind.
Sometimes I find the answers in museum archives,
sometimes in state historical societies;
at other times the answers come by thinking hard.

An Indian lady once wrote to me:
"I've always thought the *wanagi* (spirits) are
close to you. Some of your illustrations reveal that
the ancestors come to visit you in your dreams."

I love my work.
I can be at my desk from early morning until
late at night. It was the same when I was young.

Like me, do you love to write or to paint?
Do you sometimes feel disappointed
with the results of your hard work?
I also feel like that, and yet, if we are patient,
the spirits do come. Do not be discouraged.
Try again.
May the *wanagi* help you.

Paul Goble

Other Books by Paul Goble

*Iktomi and the Buffalo Skull; The Great Race; The Gift of the Sacred Dog;
Star Boy.*

About the Photographer

Gerry Perrin is a long time friend
of Paul and Janet Goble. She is
a photographer, a teacher, and a
traveller. Gerry lives in a log
house in the Saint Croix Valley
in Minnesota.

Acknowledgments

Photographs on pages 4, 19, 20, 21, 22, 23, and the back cover appear
courtesy of Janet Goble. Photographs on pages 5 and 6 appear
courtesy of Heléne Wellington. Photograph on page 6 by Elizabeth
Goble. Photograph on page 10 by author's father, Robert Goble.
Photograph on page 7 from *The Modern Harpsichord* © 1969 by
Wolfgang J. Zuckermann appears courtesy of October House, Inc.
Paintings on page 9 and photograph on page 21 appear courtesy of
Paul Goble. Book covers from *Crow Chief* © 1992 and *Iktomi and the
Ducks* © 1990 by Paul Goble on page 18 reprinted by permission of
Grolier Publishing Group/Orchard Books. Book covers by Paul Goble
on page 18 from *The Girl Who Loved Wild Horses* © 1978, *Buffalo
Woman* © 1984, *Dream Wolf* © 1990, *Death of the Iron Horse* © 1986,
Beyond the Ridge © 1989, *Lost Children* © 1993, *Love Flute* © 1992,
and *I Sing for the Animals* © 1991 by Paul Goble, reprinted with the
permission of Bradbury Press, an Affiliate of Macmillan, Inc.
Photographs on page 20 and 31 by author's son, Robert Goble.
Photographs on pages 26 and 27 appear courtesy of Nebraska State
Historical Society - Museum of Nebraska History.